Published by Creative Education
P.O. Box 227, Mankato, Minnesota 56002
Creative Education is an imprint of The Creative Company
www.thecreativecompany.us

Design and Production by The Design Lab
Printed in the United States of America

Photographs by Corbis (Bruce Adams/Eye Ubiquitous, The Art Archive, Tibor Bognár, Mark
Cooper, Abbie Enock/Travel Ink, Larry Lee Photography, Aladin Abdel Naby/Reuters,
Premium Stock, Jose Fuste Raga, Carmen Redondo, Rykoff Collection, Phil Schermeister,
Sandro Vannini, Roger Wood), iStockphoto (Karim Hesham, Tammy Peluso)

Library of Congress Cataloging-in-Publication Data
Riggs, Kate.
Egyptian pyramids / by Kate Riggs.
p. cm. — (Places of old)
Includes index.
ISBN 978-1-58341-707-2
1. Pyramids—Egypt—Juvenile literature. I. Title. II. Series.
DT63.R56 2009   932—dc22   2007051891

First edition

2 4 6 8 9 7 5 3 1

EGYPTIAN PYRAMIDS

by Kate Riggs

CREATIVE EDUCATION

THE COUNTRY of Egypt is in Africa. It sits along the Nile River. It is mostly desert. There are lots of pyramids

(*PEER-a-midz*) in the desert of Egypt. They were built for Egyptian kings called pharaohs (*FAIR-ohz*).

Crowds often gathered by the river to see the pyramids

Most of the pyramids were built about 4,000 years ago. Early pyramids did not have smooth sides. They looked like giant staircases. Then people started building pyramids with smooth sides. The pharaohs had farmers build pyramids when they weren't busy farming.

Egyptians worshiped a sun god called Ra (RAH). They believed that the pharaohs were gods, too.

Huge blocks of stone were stacked to make pyramids

The three most famous pyramids are called the Pyramids of Giza (*GEE-zah*). They were built for three kings. The tallest pyramid is as high as a 50-story building! The pyramids were made out of rocks called limestone and granite.

8

A tomb (TOOM) is a place where dead people are buried. Egyptian tombs were called mastabas (muh-STAH-buhz).

Painted coffins held the bodies of dead pharaohs

People can see what is left of mastabas near the pyramids

10

The biggest pyramid was built for a king named Khufu

Pyramids were big tombs where pharaohs were buried. The kings were wrapped up as mummies. Then they were put in the pyramids. People do not know why the pyramids are shaped like they are. Some people think they were made to look like mountains. Others think that they were made to point to heaven.

Many mummies wore fancy masks made of gold

Pharaohs' treasures went with them into the pyramids. Pharaohs were buried with gold, jewels, and other special things. But thieves stole most of the treasures from the pyramids a long time ago. There are not many tombs left that have anything inside.

12

Statues of animals and Egyptian gods were put in tombs

Egyptian sailboats are called feluccas (*FEH-loo-kahs*)

The pyramid builders used sailboats to haul blocks of limestone from quarries *to the desert.*

The capital city of Cairo is the largest city in Egypt

The pyramids are no longer by themselves in the desert. Today, the big city of Cairo (*KY-roh*) is close by.

15

The Valley of the Kings is an area of land near the Nile River. Many pharaohs were buried there.

Some pharaohs had huge statues made of themselves

Millions of people visit the pyramids every year. Only 300 people can enter one of the Pyramids of Giza each day. Too many people going in and out could hurt the pyramids.

Some pharaohs were buried with boats so that they could sail on them in the afterlife.

The world's oldest boat was found in Khufu's pyramid

People can see the pyramids from far away or up-close

Riding on camels is a good way to travel through the desert and see the pyramids.

The best time of year to visit Egypt is between December and March. It is cooler then. Other times of year, the desert is very hot.

People have ridden camels for hundreds of years

The city of Cairo can be seen from the pyramids

The Pyramids of Giza are some of the largest stone buildings in the world. They have stood for

thousands of years. People hope
that the pyramids will always
be around.

The outlines of the pyramids can be seen at sundown

glossary

afterlife
life after death; the Egyptians believed they would
have another life after they died on Earth

desert
a place that is dry because it does not get much
rain

mummies
dead bodies that have been wrapped in bandages

quarries
big, deep holes in the ground where people dig for
stone

read more about it

Chisholm, Jane, and Struan Reid. *Who Built the Pyramids?* New York: Usborne Books, 2003.

Macaulay, David. *Pyramid*. New York: Houghton Mifflin/Walter Lorraine Books, 1982.

index

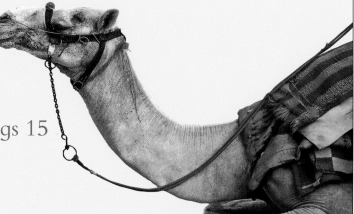